Overcome Your Interview Anxieties

Practical Tips to Reduce Interview Jitters.

For New Canadians, New Grads, and All Who Need Proven Interview Advice.

Includes Common Interview Questions With Sample Answers.

by
Leena Mary Alex, MBA, CPHR
Contributions by Shelley Goldbeck, DTM

Testimonials

"Leena's wealth of experience and practical insights are a treasure for anyone seeking new job opportunities, whether within their current organization or elsewhere. This book is an essential guide, detailing the various types of interviews one might face and offering preparation strategies. Leena empowers readers to build confidence and effectively demonstrate their qualifications using the S.T.A.R technique, making it a must-read for job applicants."
-Penny Izlakar, Director IT Strategy & Modernization program, Enbridge

"This book is an invaluable resource for any immigrant looking to advance their career in Canada and beyond. From the moment I opened it, my curiosity was piqued, and I couldn't put it down until I finished it in the comfort of my home. The language is simple, making it easy to understand. The insights provided are profound, practical, and highly relevant to today's world. The guidelines not only prepare readers for job interviews but also for the corporate environment. I highly recommend this book to every immigrant and support group."
-Ebiemi Shola-Okorodudu, Contract Conformance Specialist, Enbridge

"Leena provides practical examples of answers to common questions, job seekers' rights, and illegal interview questions in Canada. Overall, if job seekers follow the instructions in the book and complete the practical sessions, they will be better equipped to succeed in interviews."
-James Augustine, CPA-CGA, CTA

"No point missed in your quest to guide a job seeker. With the clear language and easy examples, this book would be useful for anyone in the world. In fact, I feel it should be made part of the curriculum in colleges. This book is a testimony to your many years in the industry. Wish you the very best!"
-*Mintu Mohan, Tutor, Soft Skills Trainer*

"Leena has provided a very practical guide for a 360-degree perspective of the recruitment process. Her job-seeking audience will no doubt find it incredibly useful in finding the confidence to shine in interviews and demonstrate a good potential fit in their new organizations."
-*Paul Daoust, Founder, Scio Asset Management Inc.*

Foreword

Leena, your book *Overcome Your Interview Anxieties* is more than just a guide—it's a gift to everyone navigating the often-intimidating world of job interviews. Your wisdom, drawn from personal experience and deep insight into human communication, offers not only practical strategies but also a reassuring voice for those struggling with self-doubt.

As a Toastmaster, you've always demonstrated a commitment to helping others find their voice, and this book is an extension of that passion. It provides structured guidance, real-life examples, and encouragement that make readers feel empowered rather than overwhelmed.

Your ability to break down complex ideas into relatable, actionable steps is what makes this book so impactful. It's not just about securing a job—it's about stepping into interviews with confidence, knowing that we have the tools to present our best selves.

Thank you for sharing your expertise and for making a difference in the lives of so many. Your work is an inspiration, and I have no doubt that *Overcome Your Interview Anxieties* will be a trusted companion for job seekers for years to come.

With admiration and appreciation,

Vesna Ivkovic, DTM

Introduction

Resumes, applications, and interviews… These words bring jitters to any job seeker. Mastering the art of presenting your best self and knowing the employer's expectations will maximize your chances of success.

The world we know has changed. Situations beyond our control, like a pandemic, can have an immeasurable impact on our lives. The damages are both tangible and intangible. The pandemic has changed the way we socialize, connect, or distance ourselves and even the way business is conducted around the world. Business meetings, office interactions, recruitment, training, orientation, etc., have all been impacted by the changes. With thousands of jobs negatively impacted and many more re-entering applicants, the strain also falls on recruiters. Such strain affects the recruitment process, making it longer and more arduous as candidates compete with many more applicants.

As a new immigrant, recent graduate, or someone who hasn't been interviewed in a long time, you might feel overwhelmed by the many interview questions, which can often seem more like an interrogation than a conversation.

As a job seeker and as a recruiter, I have participated in a multitude of interviews. Understandably, it's easier to be on the interviewer's side of the table. Nonetheless, I have learned powerful lessons from being on both sides of the table.

The most successful interviews I have been in are the ones where the candidate conveys poise and competency. Even highly knowledgeable candidates who cannot communicate with self-assurance can fail to impress the interview panel.

As a candidate, I have been asked several bizarre, funny, and, at times, illegal questions. It is important to know your rights in an interview. What should you divulge, and what should you withhold from the interview panel?

It can be intimidating to be surrounded by unknown people who could ask you anything. The prospect of being judged for every move you make can be nerve-wracking.

After reviewing over 50,000 resumes for a variety of positions—from accounting, geology, and engineering to management positions—and interviewing over a thousand candidates on the phone, face-to-face, and via video conferencing, I have many insights into what makes an interview successful and how to navigate one successfully, even during tough competition.

We all experience performance anxiety, especially during a job hunt. Such anxiety can hinder our ability to think, express, and articulate our thoughts.

Most people fail at interviews because they fail to prepare. It's not that they lack skills or credentials. In my experience, the main reasons candidates fail include lack of confidence, overconfidence, inability to articulate thoughts, or visible nervousness.

Nervousness is an aspect of fear that constrains the mind. When you combat this fear with thoughtful preparation, you can think and behave with a wider vision and emerge as a confident candidate.

The intent of this book is to equip you with strategies to prepare for interviews and reduce nervousness, as well as give you a glance at noteworthy responses to commonly asked questions.

Whether you are embarking on a new career or seeking a new challenge, the practical strategies and worksheets in this book will guide you in reducing interview anxiety and presenting yourself better. This book is a culmination of over 15 years of my training, learning, and experience as a recruiter.

You can send questions, feedback, or requests for interview advice to Leena@TalentSuccess.ca

Act now and own your career. I wish you success.

~Leena M Alex
www.TalentSuccess.ca

TABLE OF CONTENTS

TESTIMONIALS 3

FOREWORD 5

INTRODUCTION 7

CHAPTER ONE..17

  BELIEVE THAT YOU ARE A STRONG CONTENDER.............17

CHAPTER TWO...25

  NARRATE YOUR STORIES 25

CHAPTER THREE 33

  A VIEW FROM ANOTHER ANGLE......................................33

CHAPTER FOUR 41

  DEFINE YOUR VALUES AND VISION 41

    Writing Your Vision 44

CHAPTER FIVE 49

  TYPES OF INTERVIEWS 49

    Structured Interviews.....................................49

    Unstructured Interviews 49

    Competency-Based Interviews...............................50

    Panel Interviews 50

    Behavioral-Based Interviews...............................51

    Job Fair Interviews.......................................51

    Case Study Interviews.....................................52

Simulative Interviews..52

Informational Interviews 53

Remote Interviews..53

CHAPTER SIX..**57**

PREPARE, PREPARE, PREPARE 57

CHAPTER SEVEN **61**

RESEARCH, REHEARSE, AND REPEAT 61

Preparing for a Zoom/Skype/Phone interview.............62

Interviews with an Employment Agency 63

A Week Before the Interview....................................64

A Few Days Before the Interview 65

A Day Before the Interview......................................65

Day of the Interview..67

During the Interview..68

CHAPTER EIGHT **73**

TEN MOST COMMON INTERVIEW QUESTIONS AND SAMPLE
ANSWERS 73

Technical Questions...83

CHAPTER NINE **85**

S.T.A.R. TECHNIQUE OF ANSWERING 85

*Five Competency-Based Questions for Entry to
Intermediate Levels* 86

*Five Competency-Based Questions for Experienced and
Managerial-Level Positions* 90

CHAPTER TEN **101**

QUESTIONS TO ASK THE INTERVIEWER 101

CHAPTER ELEVEN **105**

ILLEGAL QUESTIONS IN CANADA 105

Rights at Work 106

CHAPTER TWELVE **109**

WRAPPING UP THE INTERVIEW 109

CHAPTER THIRTEEN **111**

COMMUNICATION AND LANGUAGE SKILLS....................111

CHAPTER FOURTEEN **119**

JOB SEEKER RESOURCES FOR NEW CANADIANS IN ALBERTA..119

APPENDIX 1 ....**125**

FIRST STEPS FOR NEW CANADIANS IN ALBERTA 125

Apply for a Social Insurance Number 125

Apply for Health Care (AHCIP) 125

Apply for a Driver's License....................................126

Canada Child and Family Benefits............................126

APPENDIX 2 ....**131**

Job Search Sites 131

Average Pay Scale in Canada 131

Laws on Minimum Wage and Employment Standards 131

Employment & Translation Services: 131

IQAS International Qualifications Assessment Service *131*

Licensing Bodies for Regulated Professions in Canada *131*

CONCLUSION **135**

ACKNOWLEDGMENTS..**137**

ABOUT THE AUTHOR...**138**

ABOUT CONTRIBUTING AUTHOR **139**

SHELLEY GOLDBECK, DTM.......................................**139**

We all face anxiety in our daily lives, whether it's the nervousness of speaking to strangers, public speaking, or the worry of being judged by others.

Often, the situations we feel anxious about are beyond our control.

Let's focus on a controllable factor—*you*.

Chapter One

Believe That You Are a Strong Contender

How exciting it is to receive a call from a prospective employer! When you get that call, be glad; half the battle is over. They have recognized your experience and realized that you have potential. Understand that you are a strong contender for the job.

As much as it is exciting, it can be grueling to know that you can be judged for every word you speak. A job interview places you in a high-stress situation. Your performance in the next hour or so will determine the course of your career.

Almost all adults will face a formal job interview at some point during a job search. Expressing yourself eloquently and controlling your nerves will get you closer to success.

We all experience anxiety in our daily lives—at work and while seeking new opportunities. This includes nervousness about speaking to strangers, fear of public speaking, social discomfort, and concerns about being judged by others. Anxiety can arise from apprehension about uncertain situations. In this state, it can take over one's body and mind. Since the body and mind are connected, the body quickly reacts to the anxiety in your mind by jumping into a fight-or-flight response. The rapid breathing, shaky hands, and sweaty palms can drastically narrow your mental clarity and be a resistive force to thinking, talking, and acting confidently. It is natural to feel fearful or nervous because there will be strangers in the room during the interview. They might be more knowledgeable and experienced, and their questioning style may be interrogative. Clearly, this can be unnerving and make anyone feel vulnerable.

Understandable! Let's focus on the controllable factor here—*you*.

You are only able to bring your best self forward when your body and mind are calm and at peace. Our brains are more receptive and creative when we are in a relaxed mindset.

When your mind and body are calm and relaxed, you will be able to extract your best self forward, which allows you to control how you behave while presenting your skills and abilities in the best possible light. By making simple changes in the way you approach interviews, you can make quantum leaps in finding your ideal career path.

When you submit your application, the employer sorts through hundreds of others before selecting yours. The initial review may be done by a person or assisted by data filtrations. Many companies now use applicant tracking systems (ATS) to gather and organize applications. Keep in mind that after this initial screening, only candidates who are a good fit for the job posting will be contacted.

So, start by believing that you are a strong contender. Having confidence in what you say and act conveys certainty and credibility. For you to feel confident and have ideas and thoughts flow during the conversation, the brain and body need to be in a calm and collected state. Preparation helps you to calm yourself.

An interview is a conversation on a two-way street. During the interview process, you will also make a decision whether the team and the company are ideal for you. In this conversation, reflect on your skills by providing examples from your work experience, school projects, or volunteer experience. Be approachable, personable, and polite. Overconfidence in interviews can be detrimental. Strike a balance between modesty, expertise, and confidence.

If you do not have experience in a particular area or skill, be truthful and explain some of the transferrable skills you possess to substitute those missing traits. Express your willingness to learn and master those skills. Talk about life experiences with a balance of knowledge, acquired expertise, and a strong desire to work in the role.

A few years ago, I was supporting a manager in hiring a Project Manager for his team. During the recruitment process, we screened several candidates. The manager was interested in a particular candidate due to his experience and skill set stated in the resume. On a technical basis, this candidate's credentials were ideal for the team, and we promptly set up an interview. While interviewing, the candidate displayed confidence in his knowledge and skills. But when we asked about any mistakes he had made in the past, he failed to mention any human errors or lessons learned from his mistakes during his career. The hiring manager thought that the candidate failed to create a human connection with him and decided not to proceed with the candidate.

As humans, it's inevitable that we make errors during our careers, especially in the early parts. It's our ability to accept and learn from such mistakes that make us rich in experience. My suggestion in these scenarios would be to narrate a situation where an error occurred, how you identified it, and how it was corrected. I would encourage you to talk about your learnings and how you were able to prevent those mistakes from happening again in the future.

For all questions, it is ideal to answer with examples from the past. For some, you might not remember an example immediately. It's okay to take a few moments to think and then give an appropriate answer. Some candidates ask if they can come back to the question later, and they might come up with a suitable example. Both responses are acceptable. It is quite possible that for some questions, no answer or example may cross your mind. If you draw a blank in such a situation, pause, take a few deep breaths, and think about it for a moment. Chances are, you will remember a good example when you pause and reflect. If you still cannot come up with an example, politely tell them you are unable to recollect such a scenario at this time or ask them to come back to the question later rather than give a poor example.

While speaking, pay close attention to content, structure, and delivery. Give answers deliberately and thoughtfully. Structure the answers in easy and understandable portions. Deliver your answers personably rather than sounding rehearsed.

In most interviews, you will be asked to speak about the accomplishments you're most proud of and highlight your abilities. In certain cultures, it is not considered humble to speak highly of yourself, and hence, these candidates might be reluctant to praise themselves as ideal candidates. However, an interview is the time to exemplify your knowledge and abilities to perform the potential position well. In such cases, describe your abilities as stated by your colleagues or supervisor. For instance, "My supervisor was impressed by my ability to finish reports before the due date. He has appreciated me for my time management skills. This gave him enough time to review the reports thoroughly before presenting them to upper management." In this example, the candidate's time management skills are praised by the supervisor.

Another question that is frequently asked in interviews is about conflict management. I have noticed that candidates are reluctant to speak about conflict situations they have faced. They evade the question by saying that they have never encountered conflict. In every work environment, at one time or another, differences of opinion or disagreements occur. The ability to navigate through these differences and develop solutions as a team makes you a better team player.

In the following chapters, I have provided samples of behavioral-based questions, and there is one on conflict resolution.

You can also explore some strategies to outline your values and vision. The worksheets provided will help you solidify your Unique Selling Proposition. I have included tips to minimize visible nervousness and deliver answers with confidence and without sounding over-rehearsed.

In Chapter Two, I have included resume writing tips to effectively capture the attention of recruiters. You will get exposure to a few types of interviews in Chapter Five and STAR techniques to respond effectively. The common interview questions in Chapter Eight are applicable to a multitude of positions, and each of those questions has noteworthy sample responses. The answer formats will help you practice your opening statement in a structure so that all your experience can be incorporated into a two-minute elevator speech.

Moreover, I have included a chapter on what to ask toward the end of an interview and how to effectively follow up after interviews. Chapter Fourteen is dedicated to new Canadians, with helpful resources, including information on receiving Canadian accreditation in various professions.

Your life experiences are unique to you, exactly like your fingerprint.

No one can replicate them!

Chapter Two

Narrate Your Stories

Your resume is a collection of your expertise and experience. How you write and summarize your resume speaks volumes about your personality. Weave your experiences together, adding in your notable accomplishments and credentials. This forms the basis of an impressive resume.

> Your resume speaks about your:
> - Organizational Skills
> - Language Skills
> - Attention to Detail

Do you know how much time a recruiter typically spends on reviewing a resume? Less than twenty seconds. Make every effort to make your resume stand out in appearance and make a good impression during those few critical seconds of scanning.

The first half of your resume should have 80% of your expertise and career path.

The four key elements in your resume are:
- Contact Information
- Career Summary
- Key Skills
- Experience and Education

The remaining sections cover certifications, volunteer experiences, affiliations to professional associations, publications, awards, and relevant accomplishments.

Add a professional-looking email and phone number with a clear voice message. Also, have a professional voice message recorded during the period of job search. It can be frustrating as a recruiter when you are unable to reach the candidate or leave a message. Some candidates have voicemails recorded by young children. Those messages can be unclear, or the caller can be unsure if they reached the right person. The recruiter may avoid leaving a message if they're uncertain and move on to the next candidate. To make things easier for the recruiters who try to contact you, have a clear, short, and professional-sounding voice message.

Right after your contact details on your resume, add a career summary with your expertise, the industries you have worked in, as well as key educational details. The career summary should be a condensed version of your expertise, education, and experience.

Most companies use Applicant Tracking Systems, referred to as ATS, which scans resumes and ranks them based on keywords in the job description. Recruiters also have the ability to filter resumes using certain criteria to eliminate unqualified candidates. Avoid charts, graphs, or photographs in the resume that might be difficult for the system to parse. Add those as separate documents, if necessary.

A two-page resume is ideal and easy to read for recruiters. Avoid too much formatting, underlines, brackets, different fonts, or font sizes. I recommend one font size between 10-12 for the body and 16-18 for the headings.

While creating your resume, create a rough draft by writing your responsibilities under each position. Next, think about all your great accomplishments thus far and record them chronologically. Achievements worth listing include benefits to the company, streamlining processes, time reduction measures, and risk or cost reduction. Highlight the ones that are most relevant for the targeted position. You can also use the job description and customize your application with keywords from the posting. This way, you can make sure that the system can identify those keywords from your resume.

Your accomplishments form the foundation of your resume. Adding numbers to your accomplishments, such as, "I achieved 20% above sales target within two months," shows compelling evidence of your competence.

When writing about your experiences under each position, a comprehensive list of all tasks that you completed at work is not necessary. Refine the responsibilities and add tasks that are most important to the job you are applying to. Using details of achievements brings clarity to your resume.

> Make your resume succinct and precise, ideally 1-2 pages.

Include a link to your LinkedIn profile to increase visibility. On your LinkedIn profile, you can add more details about your position. Do not include personal information such as age, family status, passport details, or driver's license number in your resume.

Listed below are some prompts for resume templates found via Google:
- <u>My Perfect Resume Free Templates</u>
- <u>Novo Resumes, Resume Templates</u>

Your resume introduces you to a company. Therefore, after reviewing many resumes and shortlisting candidates, recruiters will decide to contact candidates for an initial screening.

Recruiters and hiring managers have hectic schedules. One aspect that contributes to this is reviewing and screening each applicant. After this, they are only interested in a few candidates enough to set aside all other work and important tasks to listen to the unique stories during the interview and meet face-to-face for an in-depth conversation.

While the resume gives all the information about your experience and education, the document says little about your individuality and character. This is a good starting point for a conversation. The in-person meeting and interaction build a human connection with the interviewers. While having this decisive conversation, make a conscious effort to connect the dots and paint a comprehensive picture of your persona. The better you can articulate your stories, the better your chances of success.

All your written experiences can seem irrelevant unless you can articulate them in a way that resonates with the interviewer. Think of it this way: Your stories are a sequence of events that happened to you in the past. Intertwine your stories with your technical experience in a clear manner. Adding vivid details while narrating those anecdotes will help you build a good connection with the interviewer and establish your authenticity.

Know that your stories are unique to you, and no one can duplicate your unique life experience. They are like your fingerprints; no one else in this world has them, and no one can replicate them.

Be open in talking about your struggles and obstacles and explain how you overcame those struggles. There is no learning or success without hardships and struggles. The most important lessons come from the challenges we have faced from our life experiences. In fact, the most impressive candidates I encountered were the ones who were open about their challenges and how they turned them around as opportunities in life and learned lessons from them.

During an interview for an accounting position, I vividly remember a candidate sharing an anecdote about change management. The interview panel asked all candidates to do the following: "Give an example of a sudden change in the workplace and how you handled the change." This prompt was important in the interview since the company was going through a major organizational change at that time. The way the candidate handled change was pertinent to the success of the role.

Unfortunately, she did not have an example from her work life, but she said, "I can share a real-life experience of how I dealt with change." She and her husband were living in their hometown, very close to her parents and other relatives. Her husband worked in a sales position at a mid-sized company while she stayed home to take care of their young children. The company underwent some organizational changes and asked him to take up a position in a new city, hundreds of kilometers away from her hometown. If not, he could have lost his job. She explained, "We were left with little choice and limited time to prepare for the move. I had to leave my family, friends, and relatives at short notice." She then explained about her move from their hometown to a bigger city. In the new city, she felt the need to earn and contribute toward the family income, so she went back to school to acquire new skills to make herself employable. She started at an entry-level job in accounting, which led her to achieve her "Certified Professional Accountant" designation.

Her example was a great one to prove her adaptability and resilience in the midst of change. She clearly demonstrated her skills in coping with change. Her real-life story also culminated in showing how she succeeded in her career.

The hiring manager and I had no doubt about her transferrable skills and ability to manage changes at work. We had a new appreciation for her and offered her the position.

Similar to the example above, I suggest that you practice delivering your experiences in a positive light and focus on how you would like to portray your image.

Next, prepare answers for behavioral-based questions. Think about a few scenarios, such as managing change, conflict resolution, and effective communication. Have an example for each one of them and write them down.

Read them out loud and practice how to deliver them with clarity of voice and distinct gestures. You could also practice by recording yourself and playing it back to understand where you could improve. You are our own best critic.

**Visualize yourself from the
angle of the interviewer.**

Chapter Three

A View from Another Angle

Interviewers come with a viewpoint of finding the best fit for their team. They view how a candidate can contribute to the team by either making work easier for them or processes more efficient. They look at how the person can assimilate into the team, add value, and become an asset to the organization.

Visualize yourself from the angle of the interviewer. Do some homework on the job itself and think of how your personality will emerge while presenting yourself. Research similar postings in the industry. Look for a common thread of abilities, talents, and skills needed for those positions. Focus on the traits that are most commonly asked for. Also, check the important duties in the postings and the skills needed to complete these duties. Identify the skills and abilities you have to complete those duties effectively.

Reflect about how you would:
- Project your persona.
- Connect with your stories.
- Communicate your views, values, and vision.

To determine these, let's start by answering some questions to describe yourself and determine your goals and vision.

Take time and give some thought to these questions. Make use of the space provided to write and perhaps rewrite your answers.

List ten words to describe yourself at work. (Goal-oriented, conscientious, safety-focused, extroverted, ambitious, team player, determined, etc.)

What are the three aspects that motivate you at work?

Describe why that motivates you. (Helping clients, achieving targets, recognition from the manager, etc.)

What is the area you are most passionate about in your professional life? List the activities that bring you the most fulfillment and satisfaction. (Web design, IT, programming, teaching, etc.)

Where do you visualize yourself in the future? Include three strategies to achieve that goal. (Leading a team, obtaining a professional license, completing a degree or diploma, working for an international company, etc.)

Now, read out your answers. Listen to them, record them, talk to your confidants, and get feedback from them.

Review these goals again and revise them.

Continue to fine-tune and refine your answers.

Condense the three questions into a statement.

The combination of these three questions will potentially become your Unique Selling Proposition for the job.

____

____

____

____

____

____

____

What is most valuable to you?

How did that "value" help you to become successful?

Chapter Four

Define Your Values and Vision

Outstanding performance in any interview is backed by self-assurance.

Portray your skill set, talk about your struggles, and share how you overcame those situations. Express these with confidence and composure.

How can you obtain this composure? By having a clear set of values, vision, and unwavering passion for your line of work. Let's dedicate some time to completing this exercise based on your values and vision.

The clearer you are about your value statement, the easier it will be to elaborate on your expertise. I encourage you to define your values in your mind and do this short exercise to express your set of values.

Write down the four characteristics that have helped you achieve success in the past. (Safety focus, humility, target-oriented, honesty, loyalty, etc.)

1. __________
2. __________
3. __________
4. __________

Describe how each of these has helped with your success so far in life. (I was able to complete a project on time and accomplish the project objectives and timelines. My leadership skills helped me to motivate my team.)

____

____

____

____

____

____

____

____

____

Now, combine these two and give meaning to your values. (Due to my focus on safety and use of protective equipment, I was able to achieve 1000 hours without any incidents.)

____

____

____

____

____

____

____

The above statements tell you your value proposition and explain how you can contribute to a job and an organization.

Writing Your Vision

What is your ambition? Think of what you would like to achieve in the next five to ten years. Zoom ahead to your future and use your imagination to see what you will have achieved. Your vision stems from your perspective and life experiences. (Become a team lead or manager, complete a diploma or degree, obtain a professional certification, etc.)

1. _________
2. _________
3. _________
4. _________

Write down any practical ideas or steps to achieve these goals. Discuss or brainstorm with people you trust.

Combine the two, and you should be able to give meaning to your vision. Write down your vision for your future. Journal it in your favorite record-keeping program like Google Keep or OneNote, where you can access it quickly. (These programs are easy to use and free to download.)

Most interviews are competency-based, which focuses on obtaining information about skills that are essential for the performance of the job.

Chapter Five

Types of Interviews

Irrespective of the type of interview, they typically are an hour long, during which they can ask ten to fifteen questions, if not more. So, budget two to three minutes for each question so that there is time at the end for a discussion and for you to ask questions.

Structured Interviews

A structured interview will have a definite set of questions to elicit job-related traits. All questions will be identical for all candidates. These types of interviews are focused, objective, and tend to be predictable. Interviewers write down the answers so they can refer back to the notes to ensure that all candidates are measured by the same benchmark. I prefer structured interviews since they have consistent questions for all candidates. A lot of planning and organization goes into structured interviews. This style of interview is common for professional positions.

Unstructured Interviews

These interviews do not have prepared questions. They are spontaneous and allow an in-depth discussion about a particular topic or interest. The interviewer may bring up questions based on your past experiences. These interviews may not be the same for all candidates and lack consistency. This method of interviewing is common for retail and entry-level positions.

Competency-Based Interviews

This is one of the most popular types of interviews, which focuses on particular expertise required to be successful in the job. The desired capabilities may include adaptability, tenacity, analytical abilities, leadership qualities, interpersonal communication, motivational skills, etc. These are structured interviews with the same questions for all candidates, where the answers are rated on a scale.

Here's an example of a question about the competency of adaptability: "Tell us about a time when you had to work through a change in the organization."

Panel Interviews

When several interviewers take turns asking questions to conduct an interview, it is considered a panel interview. It can be nerve-wracking and intimidating to have several people asking questions. Preparation, knowing what to expect, and doing your homework will help strengthen your confidence in these interviews. Maintain reasonable eye contact with all members of the panel and engage with them with appropriate body language. Address the individual members by their names. Knowing their designation and looking them up on LinkedIn will help establish a good rapport with them during the conversation.

Behavioral-Based Interviews

Behavioral-based interviews are based on the following premise: "Past behavior predicts future behaviors." If you have behaved in a certain way in the past, it is likely that you will continue this behavior in the future.

They look for real-life examples from the past. Use the S.T.A.R methodology as a guideline to answer these questions.

When answering, think of:
S: An actual Situation or
T: Task you have been assigned.
A: State the specific Action taken and
R: the end Results.

If the results were not positive, share the lessons learned from that situation and how you might act differently in the future.

Job Fair Interviews

During a job fair, employers set up booths with multiple interviewers from multiple companies. These interviews can last from five minutes to an hour, depending on the interest level of the employer.

Ensure that you have an elevator pitch ready to give the interviewer to captivate their interest in your first interaction. An elevator pitch is a one to two-minute summary of your experience, education, expertise, and future goals. Project this two-minute summary with utmost conviction.

Case Study Interviews

These interviews provide an opportunity to utilize experience and reasoning skills to analyze a problem and offer the best advice within a short period of time.

More than coming up with the correct answer, it is pertinent to showcase your methodology and analytical ability. These interviews are common in engineering and IT positions.

Example: There are challenges in our invoicing department. Please see this report on the past month's invoicing tracker. What would be your approach to purchasing new software for that department? Given our current budget and the company's needs, explain your considerations while choosing this system with risks and possible benefits.

Simulative Interviews

In simulative interviews, questions are based on scenarios that an employee might face on the job in the future. The assessment helps the interviewer to know how well the candidate can organize and perform their duties.

Here's an example for a call center customer service agent: "A customer calls in very angry due to an enormous phone bill which she claims is wrong. As a customer service agent, how will you resolve this customer's issue? Explain all steps you will take in detail."

Informational Interviews

These types of interviews have gained much popularity in the last decade or so. They can be used for any level or position or even when a position does not exist. Recruiters get in touch with high-potential candidates and meet with them in an informal setting, perhaps for coffee or lunch. They have a conversation and understand the candidate's aspirations and how their skill will be a potential fit for the organization. The candidate also gets a chance to know more about the team, company, etc. These are great opportunities to expand your network and maintain rapport with a potential employer. Job seekers who normally network via LinkedIn have an advantage in getting informational interviews to know more about the industry and organization.

Remote Interviews

Skype and Zoom interviews have become very common. You can take these interviews in the comfort of your home. Some remote calls are instrumental in bringing the candidate to the next stage or even helping the hiring manager make the decision to extend the offer. So, treat all remote interviews exactly like face-to-face interviews.

Stay professional and give your undivided attention in remote interviews. Being in a quiet area with good lighting and turning off other devices helps you to focus better during these meetings. Sometimes, an overlooked aspect is your internet connectivity. It is especially important during these remote interviews to ensure yours is reliable. In Chapter Seven, I have more details on how to prepare for a remote interview.

Maintain a professional image and dress appropriately for both virtual and in-person interviews.

Practice as if you are presenting yourself in front of a panel. Keep practicing until you feel comfortable with your answers.

Chapter Six

Prepare, Prepare, Prepare

The more time and effort you spend in preparation, the more chances you have of landing an offer. You can never be over-prepared for an interview. Use as many resources and as much time as possible to prepare.

Dedicate one to two hours every day for preparation. This will be the best investment you can make for your future career. Invest in yourself to make small changes so they will multiply into bigger and better improvements. Aim for perfect progress, not perfection.

During the initial part of interviews, most companies ask what you know about them. Prepare a list of details about what impressed you about the company and why you decided to apply. If they do not ask this question in the beginning, make it a point to integrate these facts during your conversation with the potential employer.

You should also research the salary ranges of the role you are applying for in a similar industry. The base pay expectation could come up during the pre-qualifying questions or during the interview. I will provide an example of how to answer the salary question in Chapter Eight.

Once you have done your research, it is time to rehearse some of the frequently asked questions in an interview. Prepare exactly as you would present yourself in front of a panel. Refer to the commonly asked questions, prepare answers for each one, and rehearse them.

Remember, each time you practice your answers, the delivery and messaging improve. Visualize yourself in a positive manner.

Prepare by rehearsing your answers out loud in front of a mirror, a friend, or a family member. Get perspective and feedback from them about your strengths first and then areas for improvement.

Another way to review your answers is to audio or video record yourself. This will give you an idea of how long you take for each question. I suggest allocating two minutes per question in the interest of time. Practice until you are comfortable with your answers.

After practicing, ensure that the words flow effortlessly and naturally instead of sounding rehearsed. Listen to your voice and observe your body language in your recording. If English is your second language, practice so that the recruiter will clearly understand your answers. Speak slowly and clearly to ensure that the words are clear and the voice sounds confident.

If necessary, rework your tone of voice, crutch words, pauses, gestures, and level of confidence. Who else can be your best critic but yourself?

Dress for success and enhance your confidence.

**Preparation and research start
during the application process,
not a day or two before the
interview.**

Chapter Seven

Research, Rehearse, and Repeat

Preparing for an interview should start long before you are called. In fact, it should start alongside your application process. Visit the company's website to gather information about its history, values, and vision.

Make a quick note of all applications sent and facts gathered about the company.

Keep a dedicated journal or OneNote for all your applications. Make it a habit. Trust me, it helps in the long run!

Review the company's website, employee reviews, social media updates, and press releases, if any, during the application process. If those details resonate with you, mention them in your cover letter.

Understand key aspects of the company you are applying to, such as:

- Nature of Business
- History
- Core Values
- Number of Employees
- Business Vision
- Location and Branches

Other aspects to research may include access to public transit, commute time, parking, benefits provided, community involvement, professional development support, growth opportunities, company expansion plans, etc.

Sometimes, an employer may call spontaneously in response to your application, and you might be caught off guard. They might ask a few questions, and there may not be ample time to prepare at that instant. The research you did earlier will pay off and help you to answer their questions confidently. Having prepared your vision and value statement gives you a good start for this conversation. Keeping these statements on your device can be helpful so you can review them quickly.

If you're in a public place when a potential employer calls, be aware of your surroundings. Find a quiet place or suggest they call back in a few minutes.

Preparing for a Zoom/Skype/Phone interview

With the advent of technology and post-pandemic closures, most companies conduct phone interviews or video conferences. Treat these interviews exactly as in-person interviews. Before the interview, prepare by having a copy of your resume and job posting at hand and find a quiet and well-lit room. Ensure that your internet connection is stable and that the device has sufficient charge and is in a stable position, preferably not handheld. Other devices should be turned off to minimize distractions. During the interview, maintain clarity of voice, use professional language, and dress for success.

Interviews with an Employment Agency

Staffing agencies can open doors to a variety of positions, including contract, temporary, and permanent.

If you've applied to an employment agency, they collect information and usually do a phone or face-to-face interview to understand your communication skills, experience, and goals before presenting this to the potential employer. Since they present your resume and information to the company representative, be open and upfront about your goals, expertise, and experience. They will be representing the company and acting as a bridge between the employer and the candidate. They'll have more information about the role and the employer. At times, the company may be confidential until they call for a direct interview with the company. Gather as much information about the job and company as possible at that time.

Staffing agencies should not ask for a social insurance number (SIN), date of birth, or other personal information before making an offer. The company pays them to find a suitable candidate, so they do not take any money from candidates. If an agency charges you money to find a job, that is unlawful. Do not engage further with that agency.

Follow up with your agent a week or so after the interview to get feedback and updates. Record the interview dates and information shared. Since agencies interview for multiple positions for many companies, it is imperative to follow up with them. If that position doesn't pan out, ask them about other opportunities.

A Week Before the Interview

Some companies call a week before the interview date; some call only a couple of days before. If you have a week before the interview, consider yourself fortunate. Set aside at least one to two hours per day for preparation; it will be the best investment of your time.

The first step is to research the company. Look at the company website, social media, press releases, employee reviews, benefits they offer, charities they support, community involvement, or any significant project they have undertaken in the recent past. Also, understand the company values and vision. Then, distinguish key values that resonate with you. Sift through your own resume and experiences and highlight your attributes that will add value to the company.

Secondly, print a copy of the job posting. Highlight the job responsibilities and credentials that you possess. Make notes beside it. Think of examples of where you've done those duties or utilized the skills. List real-life instances of when you've done those duties on separate paper and attach it to the job posting. Take it with you for the interview. If necessary, refer to these notes. Picture yourself answering questions. Though this might seem like a small thing to do, it can work wonders while you're in the interview.

Make an opening and closing statement about your expertise and how it matches the position. Toward the end of the interview, as the meeting is wrapping up, add a sentence or two to summarize your Unique Selling Proposition. This will remind them about your expertise. Practice those statements out loud.

Print your opening statement, Unique Selling Proposition, value, and vision statements. Review and verbalize them. Visualize yourself performing well in the interview.

A Few Days Before the Interview

Before the interview, review what other companies are looking for in a similar position and what the most sought-after attribute is in the role you have applied for. Focus on how that attribute resonates with you. Make notes of where you were able to capitalize on such attributes. Write down your ambition and career goals. Fill your mind with positive thoughts about yourself and your abilities to perform the job. Practice deep breathing and calming yourself in these high-stress situations.

A Day Before the Interview

A day before the interview, review all the notes, including the research of the company, the job posting, value and vision statements, the duties you have completed, your most important attributes, and quantifiable real-life examples of your experience. At this point, have your opening and closing statements memorized.

Print out the location and contact person. Check how long it takes to travel to the location and budget 10-20 minutes extra for the trip. It's better to be early than late. Be well nourished and hydrated, and get good sleep the night before. Meditate and connect with the universe to improve focus. Do what you can to unwind your mind. Fill yourself with positive thoughts about your performance. Feel confident, enthusiastic, and in control.

Make a conscious effort to dress professionally. Although not all employers require employees to dress formally, it's best to err on the side of caution and dress for success. Avoid very bright colors or excessive jewelry. Try on your clothes and shoes the day before. Ensure that your clothes are clean and your shoes polished. Since many workplaces are scent-free, steer clear of strong perfumes.

Certain types of cuisines use many aromatic spices, the smell of which remains in the home and infuses with clothing. This smell can be perceived as a bad odor, especially to people sensitive to smells. Ensure your clothes are free from food or cooking odor. One way to avoid food odors is to place them in a dryer and run a cycle for about twenty minutes. Another way is to use a lightly scented disinfectant spray like Lysol or Febreze.

A colleague of mine, who is sensitive to smells, had an interview with a candidate whose coat carried the scent of spices. She ended the interview within minutes because she couldn't tolerate the odor. After the candidate left, she even sprayed Lysol in the room to eliminate the smell. Unfortunately, the candidate missed the chance to showcase all his skills during that interview.

Day of the Interview

On the day of the face-to-face interview, arrive early, well-dressed, and poised. Wear comfortable clothes and shoes.

Arriving too early can be inconvenient for the interviewer, as they might be wrapping up another meeting or interview. It's ideal to arrive about 10 to 15 minutes before your scheduled time.

While waiting to be called into the reception, you can keenly observe the atmosphere and office interactions. Usually, the values and vision will be shown in the reception area. There could also be awards received by the company on display. Take an interest in them, and during the meeting, it could be a good conversation starter. Be courteous to everyone, including security, receptionists, and interviewers. Bring a work bag to carry a bottle of water, Kleenex, a notebook and pen to write notes, and a copy of your resume, job posting, and any additional certificates or proud professional accomplishments.

Have a few motivating statements in your mind, such as:
"It's going to be okay."
"I will shine."
"I am competent."
"I have potential."

"I am successful."

Believe in your unique skills and abilities. Silently practice your opening and closing statements.

Maintain a good posture or strike a power pose even while waiting in the reception area. Take slow, deep breaths and gaze upward while waiting to reduce the nerves. This helps regulate your breathing and saturate your body with oxygen. This helps you to remain calm, think better, and widen your vision! This will help you to dispel nervousness.

During the Interview

When the interviewer greets you at reception, smile warmly, shake their hand, and thank them for selecting you for an interview.

Professionalism is a must, not a nice-to-have, for all interviews. Do not use foul language or swear words. Doing so can be perceived as having a lack of respect for the panel.

The first five to ten minutes of the interview are critical. Some recruiters form a mental framework for the candidate during that time and make their decision based on the opening statement; hence, it is pertinent to have a strong one.

The interviewers pay attention to non-verbal communication and body language to unravel your answers. Maintain eye contact with all panelists. Use pleasing body language to indicate you are open and accepting. Crossed hands and arms are perceived as closed off, while open palms indicate a welcoming nature. Use hand gestures in your conversion, especially when indicating a shape, size, or direction or emphasizing certain points.

You might be nervous about the interview. Take deep, slow, and conscious breaths to calm your nerves and think positively. Maintain an upright, confident posture during the interview. It is a quick and easy way to get rid of the nerves, and you can do it without making anyone aware of it. Ensure that your fear or nervousness is not visible or evident. If your nervous behavior is noticeable, it can subconsciously make the interviewer uncomfortable, too. They have pressure on themselves in terms of timelines and to land the best candidate. Remember, they want you to do well during the interview. Make it easy for them to arrive at a decision faster.

During the interview, it is pertinent to validate any details on your resume with solid examples. Ensure that you are familiar with all parts of your resume since questions can arise from any part of it. Use figures and numbers to support your experience.

Radiate confidence and be graceful during the interview. They are ready to give their precious time to listen to your stories. Always be truthful. Be prepared for follow-up questions. Articulate your experiences while reflecting on your unique personality. Overall, make this time worthwhile for both parties.

Provide real-life examples to support your credibility, adaptability, and collaboration skills. Do not sound robotic or rehearsed. Avoid overused words such as "hard-working," "punctual," "excellent communication skills," etc. This is the minimum requirement for all employees, and they already expect this from you!

Demonstrate kindness and be confident in the choice of your words. Add humor when possible. It will help alleviate some pressure for both parties in the room. Picture the interviewers as kind people who truly want to listen to you and help you succeed.

All interviews might not result in offers. You can improve your level of confidence and learn from past mistakes. It is important to make a good impression on the panel so they can consider you for a future position.

Answer all questions honestly.

Do not sound over-rehearsed. Show excitement in your voice and confidence in your body language.

Chapter Eight

Ten Most Common Interview Questions and Sample Answers

After exchanging pleasantries, the employers usually ensure that candidates are comfortable before they dig into their list of questions. They may ask about the weather, traffic outside, or any current events. You can even start the conversation with what you observed in the reception area, such as company awards or publications. Prepare a few talking points for small talk. Refrain from saying that you are nervous or anxious.

Remember that the interview is typically an hour, and the timeframe is rather limited to explain all your experiences. Provide short, specific answers to the questions asked. Brevity is key when balancing your time. The interviewers generally ask questions that are most relevant to the job duties. Ask them if you have answered the question or if they need more details.

Demonstrate your ability to be flexible and weave this into your responses. The post-pandemic era is one where flexibility, adaptability, and remote work would be seen as superior skills in the work environment. All team members may not be in one location, and you may not have the opportunity to see each other frequently. Due to remote work arrangements, body language, human interactions, and daily office conversations may be absent. Despite all these changes, employees must prove their productivity and achieve targets and goals. This could present challenges for supervisors and managers when completing performance appraisals, ensuring a congenial team dynamic, and ultimately achieving the goals of the team. They will be seeking individuals who can integrate remote work arrangements and adapt to changes quickly.

According to a LinkedIn survey, 92% of talent professionals believe that soft skills are as important, if not more important, than technical skills when making hiring decisions. For each question, they will be observing soft skills like adaptability, ability to work remotely, interpersonal skills, punctuality, etc.

No matter the position, there are some common questions in every interview. I have included a few here. Take inspiration from these answers, but do not replicate them. Share your own experiences related to each example.

1. <u>**Tell Us More About Yourself**</u>

This is an important icebreaker question and is often asked in interviews. When answering this question, they perceive how well you communicate, your knowledge of the job, your holistic experience, and what you look forward to in the position. In less than two minutes, summarize your experience, education, and industries you have worked in and highlight your soft skills. Use the following format to answer this question.

Example: My experience spans over _____ years in the _______ area, specifically in _______. I started my career in ______ as ______, during which I learned more

____

about _______. Over the past year/s, I gained valuable experience in _____ and had the opportunity to work in industries such as ____. Most recently, my experience in ______ has given me exposure to _____ and ______, which will be helpful in this position. I consider myself an expert in ____ area. Also, as an avid ______, I got the opportunity to ______.

By including a few details not found on the resume, you can instantly engage the interview team with what sets you apart. Steer clear of strong political opinions, religious beliefs, or anything that could be considered polarizing. Make it simple for them to see your skills as transferable to the position and recognize your potential.

Employers in Canada are not allowed to ask personal questions pertaining to age, religion, family status, or ethnicity. The interview process is to determine competency and specific skills. Take this as a great opportunity to leave a mark on a potential employer with your positive personality. Think long-term!

The goal is to emerge as a confident candidate so the employer has a lasting impression of your abilities. If you are not selected for the current role, they could call you back if you leave a great impression. Once, I had the opportunity to call back a candidate who was rejected for a position originally. This was because the candidate left us a lasting impression with their personality fit and positivity during the interview. We were convinced that the company could benefit from their presence. I was delighted to call back and offer a position. I felt very positive knowing that they would indeed thrive in that role.

2. **Walk Us Through Your Resume**

This question is also a commonly asked icebreaker. Rather than repeating everything on the resume, add more details to keep the conversation interesting.

Example: I started my career at _________ after graduating from ________. During the earlier part of my career, I focused on _________. Soon, I became proficient in _______, which helped me to get a role in _______. There, I expanded my knowledge and skills in ______. My role at _______ was a learning experience professionally because of ______. In spite of _____, I succeeded in that role. In my current role, I thrived in ____, and at this juncture, I am looking for a change because of ______.

This format will help you elaborate on your expertise, experience, interests, career path, and why you are looking for a change at this time. Adding personal interests will also give you a chance for some small talk.

3. **Why Do You Want to Work for Us?**

The employer is curious to know what you have learned about the company and why you decided to apply for this position.

As mentioned in an earlier chapter, it is important to research the company. I have a three-part answer to this question.

- Mention what impresses you about the company, industry, reputation, or nature of business.
- Describe why the role suits you and how it matches your experience.
- Add a personal touch to what you have read or heard about the company that resonates with you.

This answer will include what you like about the company and how your expertise can contribute to the position.

4. <u>What Is Your Proudest Professional Accomplishment?</u>

Most employers ask about your proud achievements to determine what you are capable of and how you can express it without being arrogant.

They do so to understand your abilities and what you think of as an accomplishment. The scale of achievements can differ depending on the circumstances and each person's potential.

Think about a goal you were able to achieve despite obstacles. Refer to examples you rehearsed ahead of time, factoring in the strengths that helped you achieve this feat with numbers and timelines.

Example: In my previous role as communications lead, I suggested ideas to increase the website viewership. I suggested adding articles and videos to the website weekly about our company's products and also showcasing an employee. My manager approved the project. Within four weeks of implementing this project, our viewership increased by over 35%. This was possible due to my planning skills, collaboration with the team, and time management.

5. <u>Tell Us About Your Weaknesses</u>

Though this can appear unflattering, most interviewers ask this since they know that all people have areas for development. They prefer to hear about your areas for improvement in your own words. All people come with strengths and weaknesses, and it's only two sides of the same coin. Personally, I prefer the question, "What are your areas for improvement?" When you get the question on weakness, try to answer with the areas you could improve. The key to answering this question is to be self-aware of the skills you can work on and what you can do to improve them. Moreover, it alludes to the fact that we are all a work-in-progress.

We're aware of some of our weaknesses, and we're blind to others. If you receive feedback from one of your peers or supervisors, take it seriously since others can often see things that we cannot.

Thoroughly evaluate your skills and abilities. Prepare and write down a response that allows you to discuss a skill you're still developing or one in which you are working to gain expertise.

This could be time management skills, accounting, or public speaking. Make sure that these skills are not quintessential to this position. Mention any steps taken to achieve those skills, like taking evening courses or online classes or even reading or researching more about the topic. This shows you are aware of your areas for improvement and have taken steps toward working on them.

Example: Earlier in my career, I had the habit of taking on too many tasks at one time. This, unfortunately, led to unmet deadlines. I had to learn some painful lessons from the lost time and unmet goals. After taking a time management course, I learned to estimate timelines for each task, delegate duties, and communicate the progress of my assignments to my manager and the team. This has helped me with my time management and communication with the team and created an appreciation for the set timelines, too. Now, 95% of my projects are done on time or before the deadline. This is due to my continued efforts to improve my time management skills.

6. Why Are You Leaving Your Current Position?

This question is intended to understand your focus on different aspects that led you to make the decision to start your job search. Give some thought to what exactly you are looking to gain in the next position. It could be professional, such as taking on greater responsibilities, or personal reasons, such as moving to be closer to family. Compile a thoughtful answer with one or two main points. Place emphasis on the new opportunity, the potential to acquire other skills, and the high level of interest in the company. Explain the answer in a way that highlights your desire to gain more responsibility and experience, obtain a new skill set, change career direction, etc.

Ensure that you do not say anything that could defame your previous employer or leader. Other legitimate reasons for leaving a position might include restructuring, reduced workload, or the role no longer having enough work to sustain the position. If a large number of people were laid off at that time due to restructuring, be sure to mention those reasons as well.

Example: In my current position, I have achieved a good rapport with my team, increased the sales of the product by 25%, and achieved the "Salesperson of the Year" award last year. My focus is now more on product development and research. This new position will allow me to use my experience in building client relationships by taking their feedback and implementing my creativity when making new products. For the past year, I have been taking online courses to improve my skills in this area.

7.   <u>Why Is There a Gap in Your Employment?</u>

Gaps in employment can occur due to several factors, including layoffs, a shortage of work, the end of a contract, restructuring, termination, resigning to move to a different city, changes in career path, returning to school, extended maternity leave, or taking care of a loved one. Clearly state the reasons and explain how you utilized the gap to benefit personally or professionally.

Example: There was a gap in my employment from 2015 to 2016, during which I stayed home to care for my mother. She needed constant care after surgery, and I couldn't assign this important duty to anyone else. During this time, I took courses to upgrade my skills in web design and development. I also worked on putting together a family tree project with pictures of all my family members, which I gifted to my mom.

8. What Do You Plan to Accomplish in the First Three Months?

Formulating a 30/60/90-day plan for your new job will be immensely beneficial for both you and your employer. It's proof that you have thought through and visualized yourself in this role.

Example: During the first 30 days, my focus will be on people, processes, and procedures. I want to familiarize myself with the internal systems and team members. Every company has a unique culture, workflow, and team dynamic. I'll strive to acclimate myself to this unique culture, understand the workflow, and be a part of the team.

Within the first 60 days, I'll become accustomed to the people on my team and get to know other teams we work closely with. I'll familiarize myself with the company's Standard Operating Procedures and internal software systems and adapt to the team's unique culture. It will also be a time to build trust and gain confidence.

During the first 90 days, I will become well-trained in the internal systems and techniques and learn best practices to improve productivity. I'm confident that I will become efficient and productive in my work within that time frame.

9.   <u>Where Do You See Yourself in Five Years?</u>

It is important to have goals for the future and career plans, which include professional development. Include details about a career trajectory you anticipate. This may involve developing certain skills and acquiring knowledge in your area.

Example: As an HR professional, in the next five years, I intend to gain more well-rounded experience in human resources, including performance appraisal, workforce planning, training & orientation, and succession planning. I can then utilize this experience to coach and mentor junior HR professionals. I aspire to be a leader in the next five years.

10. <u>What Are Your Expectations for Annual Salary?</u>

All positions have a budgeted salary allocated by the department. Interviewers ask this question to understand your knowledge of the position and see if that matches their budget and affordability. If you're unsure of the ranges, research salaries of similar roles on Indeed Salaries or Payscale.ca. Depending on the previous position, level of expertise, and industry standards, give them a range and let them know you are flexible.

Example: The salary range I have in mind is between $X and X annually, based on the salary ranges of similar positions at this level. However, I'll be flexible to fit your budgeted salary range and company needs.

Do not leave this question unanswered. It's best to answer with the research you have completed or your desired salary range. Interviewers may be confused if you don't have a salary range in mind. This is also part of your preparation.

Technical Questions

For engineering and technical positions, they will likely ask technical questions related to the position. In addition to the above questions, always prepare for some technical ones. It's a great idea to bring a portfolio of your work—including drawings, outlines of projects, etc.—to demonstrate if such a question arises. This is also indicative of your passion and interest in your work.

Most importantly, answer all questions truthfully and honestly. Avoid sounding overly rehearsed. Show excitement in your voice and confidence in your body language. Your positive personality should shine through in your answers.

Use a journalistic approach to answering competency-based questions: "Who, What, Where, When, and How."

Chapter Nine

S.T.A.R. Technique of Answering

As mentioned earlier in Chapter Five on different interview types, behavioural-based interview techniques are commonly used in interviews. Interviewers look for S.T.A.R. responses to their questions. To answer them accurately, follow the S.T.A.R. methodology.

The S.T.A.R. technique of answering a question requires the following parts:

- Situation – The event or incident
- Task – Your role in the situation
- Action Taken – Details of your actions
- Results – The end results of your actions

Remember, there are no right or wrong answers to behavioral-based questions. The interviewers are looking for examples from the past and how you acted in certain situations. For most behavioral-based interview questions, it is best to use a journalist approach of "Who, What, Where, When, and How."

If the question is confusing or too complex, ask the interviewer to repeat it or explain more in detail. If a specific situation has not occurred to you, be upfront and let them know. You can also ask for another scenario. If no specific example comes to mind, think for a few moments or politely ask them to come back to this question later.

Five Competency-Based Questions for Entry to Intermediate Levels

1. <u>Interpersonal Skills</u>

Tell us about a time when you demonstrated interpersonal skills while working in a team.

This question is pertinent if the candidate works closely with people in a multi-disciplinary environment.

Example: I enjoyed working in a team of ten people on an assignment for about four months. Our objective was to save the company 10% of costs in production. (Situation & Task)

I set up a plan to lead the team, presented it to our manager, and had it approved. I worked through some suggested modifications along the way with the team. The input from all team members was valuable. (Action)

Despite our limitations and obstacles, we successfully completed the project. We finished on time and saved the company 15% (about $10,000 within a month), exceeding our target of 10%. This was a significant success for the team. We achieved this through a collaborative work group focused on planning and execution and dedicated to accomplishing our goals. (Final Outcome)

2. <u>Receiving Feedback</u>

Tell us about a time you made a mistake at work and how you resolved it.

The intention of this question is to know how you rise above the occasion and take responsibility to rectify an error. However, many candidates are caught off guard and get flustered when asked this.

Everyone makes mistakes and errors. It's important to learn from them and take measures to avoid repeating them. I've seen some interviewers heavily emphasize this question to understand whether you take responsibility for your mistakes, accept feedback, apologize, and take measures to correct your misdoings. Be honest about a mistake, understanding that no one is perfect. Think of one you committed and how you were able to take full responsibility when correcting it. Secondly, indicate what you learned or how you could have handled it differently if you were in the same situation.

Example: In one of my positions, I missed a deadline, which resulted in a loss of business for the company. There were some controllable and uncontrollable factors that contributed to this. I analyzed them and made a report on the factors that led to missing the deadline. This made me realize where I had gone wrong and how I could have rectified the error. I apologized for my mistake and immediately took measures to fix the issue. I communicated to my supervisor about the error and the measures I'd taken to prevent it from happening in the future. We had an open discussion, and he suggested how I could make up for the missed deadline. After that incident, I made sure that I managed my time and finished assignments well before the timeline. My supervisor appreciated my progress when I completed the next project before the deadline.

3. <u>Conflict Resolution</u>

Tell us about a time when you had to handle a conflict at work.

Conflict arises at one time or another in every organization. It's important to acknowledge that it exists, face it, handle it with reason, and move on.

The interviewer would like to hear how you navigated a conflict situation with grace and resilience. The maturity you show in such conflicts will help you to manage other situations effectively.

Example: There was one person on my team when I was the marketing lead who was consistently late in completing tasks, which affected my work. This created a conflict in my mind, and I was unable to communicate this to her. I soon realized that my relationship with her was suffering, so I set up a meeting with her to explain the nature of our assignment, which was dependent on finishing tasks on time so we could move ahead and finish the entire assignment. She explained another project to me that she was involved in, which had similar timelines. I listened to her perspective without judgment and asked her for some suggestions to work around the problem. We both discussed some solutions. She understood the urgency of the situation and asked for a few more days to complete the task. I handled a potential conflict with respect and ensured that there was a resolution. I was able to get the task completed in a few days.

What I learned in this situation was the importance of understanding others' perspectives and finding solutions to move forward.

4. <u>Applied Learning</u>

Describe a new skill you had to learn at work and how you learned it.

This prompt is given to understand how quickly you're able to gain knowledge and put in effort to master a skill.

Example: In my last position as a telephone sales agent, I had to quickly learn the regional boundaries. This helped me to explain the regions to the customer in detail. I had a chart in front of me with the geographical areas while speaking to them.

On each call, I verified the area before I talked to them. I read through the document every day before work to familiarize myself with it. Within two weeks, I was well acquainted with all the areas and boundaries. This helped me improve my confidence level while talking to the customer and meeting my sales target.

5. <u>Building Relationships</u>

Tell us about a time when you had to build a good relationship with an external client.

Building good working relationships is essential in any work environment. By extending a good interpersonal relationship, people feel valued and appreciated.

Your ability to ask questions, understand expectations, and meet and exceed expectations should be demonstrated by answering this prompt.

Example: When I took over the last position as client relations lead, I made sure to contact all the clients in my area for a check-in and asked if they faced any challenges with our product or delivery.

We had some candid conversations with one client about how to improve product delivery. After gathering all the information and compiling the data, I relayed this back to my manager with several suggestions. Within two months, we were able to implement three suggestions that emerged to improve our delivery. All our clients benefitted from those changes.

Five Competency-Based Questions for Experienced and Managerial-Level Positions

1. <u>Giving Feedback About Performance</u>

Q: Describe a time when you had to give feedback on the under-performance of a team member.

By posing this prompt, the interviewer wants to understand your ability to track team performance and provide essential feedback to team members.

Example: During the first part of the year, we set goals for the team through a series of discussions with each team member, focusing on both individual and collective objectives. The intention behind these conversations was to ensure that everyone had clear, attainable goals that aligned with both their personal development and the broader team objectives. I made it a point to follow up on the progress regularly, scheduling monthly check-ins with each team member to understand how they were advancing toward their goals. These meetings were an opportunity to review their progress and offer guidance, encouragement, and feedback where necessary.

As the months went by, I noticed that one particular employee was struggling to meet the goals we had set for him. Despite the fact that the rest of the team seemed to be progressing well, his output consistently fell short of expectations. During our monthly meetings, I took the time to give him constructive feedback on the work he had completed and engaged in an open discussion about any roadblocks he was facing. In one such meeting, I specifically asked if there was anything I could do to help him achieve his goals. It was then that he revealed a critical issue I hadn't been aware that he had been dealing with ergonomic challenges in his workspace. These issues were causing him discomfort and were preventing him from producing his best work.

The revelation came as a surprise to me because, up until that point, I had been unaware of the physical challenges he was experiencing. However, I immediately recognized the seriousness of the situation and assured him that I would take swift action to resolve the matter. I reached out to our health and safety department and scheduled a meeting to address his ergonomic concerns. They were quick to respond and assessed the situation within days, identifying adjustments that needed to be made to his workstation to alleviate the physical discomfort he had been experiencing. Within two weeks, the necessary corrections were implemented, and his working conditions were significantly improved.

Once the ergonomic issues were resolved, I kept a close eye on his performance and was pleased to see a marked improvement within just a month. With the physical barriers out of the way, he was able to meet his targets and perform at the level we both knew he was capable of. His output not only reached the expected standard but also began to exceed our original goals. Reflecting on this experience, I'm grateful that I took action at the right time by being proactive in inquiring about his performance.

This situation reinforced the importance of asking the right questions and showing genuine curiosity about the well-being of team members. By creating a space where employees feel comfortable sharing personal challenges, I was able to provide meaningful support that had a direct impact on performance. This experience emphasized that leadership is not just about managing tasks but also about caring for the people who carry them out. By being attentive and acting swiftly, I was able to help my team member overcome a significant obstacle and improve his overall performance, which contributed to the success of the entire team.

2. <u>Technical/Professional Knowledge</u>

Describe a complex multidisciplinary project you have worked on. What was your role? Explain the lessons learned from it.

This question targets technical knowledge and your ability to collaborate with others before effectively utilizing the acquired knowledge. Choose a recent project and provide as many specifics as possible.

Example: As a project manager, I had the opportunity to lead a team of twenty individuals, which included experts from technical, IT, design, and construction disciplines. This diverse team was responsible for a significant project: the integration of a new system into an existing application, which spanned a period of ten months. The nature of the project demanded a high level of coordination and collaboration, as it involved multiple disciplines working together to achieve a common goal. This complexity presented numerous challenges, but it also made the project an invaluable learning experience, which I thoroughly enjoyed.

One of my key responsibilities was developing a comprehensive project plan. I meticulously outlined each phase of the project, ensuring that every task was clearly defined and that objectives and deadlines were set accordingly. I assigned duties to team members based on their expertise, ensuring that everyone had a clear understanding of their roles and responsibilities. This detailed planning helped streamline the workflow, allowing for effective communication and coordination between the teams involved.

During the course of the project, I also had the opportunity to expand my skill set by learning new software programs that were essential for managing the project's technical aspects. Time management was crucial, as the project involved tight deadlines and required the efficient allocation of resources. I worked closely with the various teams, ensuring that milestones were met and addressing any challenges that arose. My ability to manage these complexities helped keep the project on track.

Ultimately, the project was completed successfully, both on time and on target. This achievement was a testament to the collaboration between the different teams and the effective management of the various tasks involved. The experience enhanced my technical and management skills and reinforced the importance of teamwork, communication, and adaptability in delivering successful outcomes.

3. Planning and Organizing

Tell me about a time when you were accountable for shaping assignments, schedules, and timelines for a project you were managing.

This prompt is meant to determine the depth of responsibilities and strength of the teams you have managed. All projects may not go as per the desired plan. Try to include the challenges you had to face and how you were able to overcome them successfully.

Example: As a team leader, one of my primary responsibilities was carefully assessing the project's scope and determining the tasks that needed to be completed. I began by identifying the necessary equipment, materials, and personnel required for each specific task. This planning stage was crucial in laying a strong foundation for the project, ensuring that each element was properly aligned with the project's goals. After gathering these resources, I allocated time for the completion of each task based on their complexity and urgency. This helped me develop a realistic timeline for the entire project. By structuring the work this way, I ensured that tasks were approached in an organized manner.

To manage the complexities of the project, I focused on breaking down large tasks into smaller, manageable pieces. This approach not only made the work more digestible for the team but also allowed us to utilize the available resources efficiently. By segmenting the work into smaller steps, it became easier to track progress and adjust our approach where necessary. This breakdown also made it possible to delegate specific tasks to team members whose skills were most suited to them, thus maximizing individual contributions toward the project's success.

However, as with most projects, challenges arose. One major obstacle was the unavailability of certain materials and shortages in labor, which caused delays in the project timeline. These unexpected setbacks required me to adapt and adjust our original plan. I gathered the team, and we held discussions to brainstorm potential solutions. Instead of making decisions unilaterally, I presented various options to the team and actively involved them in the decision-making process. Their input was valuable, as they brought different perspectives and ideas, which ultimately helped us find the best way forward. By incorporating their suggestions, we were able to make strategic changes that allowed us to move ahead despite the obstacles.

Throughout the project, persistent follow-up and communication were key. I ensured that regular check-ins were held with the team to stay updated on task progress and address any emerging issues. This ongoing engagement helped us stay focused on the tasks at hand and adhere to the revised timelines we had set after our pivots. Through consistent monitoring and adjustments, we were able to keep the project on track and maintain momentum despite the hurdles we faced. Overall, the experience reinforced the importance of adaptability, collaboration, and effective communication in overcoming challenges and delivering successful project outcomes.

4.   <u>Strategic Decision-Making</u>

Describe how you have involved other people in decision-making.

It is imperative for a manager to involve the team in decision-making to create a sense of buy-in for the team. Teams feel more engaged and valued when they are in the loop on decision-making.

Example: In my previous role, I actively involved my team in selecting new software for our department. To begin, I organized a meeting to identify the inefficiencies and gaps in our current system that were hindering our success. Next, I assigned team members specific tasks, such as researching the costs, benefits, and potential risks of various software options. Once the research was complete, we came together as a team to evaluate the choices, ensuring they aligned with our long-term goals and vision. Ultimately, we selected the most efficient and cost-effective software, which significantly improved time management and overall efficiency.

By engaging the team in this decision-making process, I demonstrated a collaborative leadership style, which fosters active participation and buy-in from team members. This approach not only improves outcomes but also boosts engagement and commitment to the work. Collaboration is a highly valued skill in senior-level roles, as it helps build strong, cohesive teams that work together to achieve shared goals.

5. <u>Work Habits and Productivity</u>

What have you done to maintain productivity in the midst of distractions and changing priorities?

Maintaining focus and energy is important amidst change. Changes are inevitable in any organization, and having an attitude of adaptability and acceptance toward them makes any transitions smoother.

Example: I maintain high levels of productivity through a disciplined approach driven by determination and focus. I prioritize timelines and consistently deliver strong output by staying organized and committed to my work. Even when priorities shift, I ensure clear communication with my manager to keep her updated on my progress. I also seek feedback from peers and my leader to refine my work, all while staying focused on current projects.

My primary goal is to meet my targets efficiently, maintaining a steady pace and open lines of communication with both my manager and team members. I aim for a high level of effectiveness in everything I do. Additionally, I support my productivity by incorporating regular exercise and mindfulness into my routine, which helps sustain my energy and focus.

**Ask open-ended questions.
Maintain rapport and positivity
while doing so.**

Chapter Ten

Questions to Ask the Interviewer

The interviewer usually provides an opportunity at the end for you to ask questions. If they do not, politely inquire if you may ask a few. Take advantage of this chance to clarify any doubts and pose some thoughtful questions.

Do your homework on addressing any questions you might have had during the research or the interview itself. Ask open-ended questions. Maintain rapport and positivity while doing so.

Examples:

1. Could you describe your leadership style?
2. Can you share more details about the structure of your team or department?
3. How long is the training period, and who will be responsible for training the new employee?
4. What does success in this role look like to you?
5. What would you say is the most challenging part of this position?
6. What qualities contribute to your team's success?
7. What were the key strengths of the previous person in this role?
8. What soft skills are you prioritizing in the ideal candidate for this position?
9. Are there any professional development opportunities within the team?

10. Which skills and abilities are essential for
success in this role?

Asking questions that are important to you will help you get a good understanding of the company culture, team environment, potential challenges, daily routine, reporting structure, software used, training given, and the people whom you will be working with closely. It indicates your interest and commitment to the job. Additionally, ask if any of your responses to the questions require further clarification.

In certain cultures, it is not polite to question authority or ask questions to the interview panel. However, by asking some questions related to the position, the interview panel will appreciate your inquisitiveness. The questions are also indicative of your research on the organization.

Sound polite and curious by starting with:
"I am curious to know…"
"What do you think…"
"Would you be able to explain more about…"

In my experience, candidates who ask thought-provoking questions based on their research about the company and their area of work often impress the hiring manager. These questions and how they are asked make a huge impact on the decision made by the interview team. Conclude with your closing statement. Finish strong and confidently.

Unless there is a bona fide requirement, personal questions are illegal. Interview questions should be designed to assess a candidate's ability to perform the job effectively.

Chapter Eleven

Illegal Questions in Canada

Questions should be intended to understand the candidate's ability to perform the job well. The interviewer is forbidden from asking questions relating to age, race, ethnicity, religion, creed, family status, marital status, sexual orientation, financial status, place of origin, or physical disability unless there is a bona fide requirement for that job. With very few exceptions, none of the following questions should be asked in an interview.

As a candidate, you should be aware of illegal questions that might be asked by the employer.

Examples of illegal questions during the interview:

1. When did you arrive in Canada?
2. What is your family status?
3. Are you married or single?
4. How many children do you have?
5. Do you intend to have more children?
6. What is your mother tongue?
7. Where were you born?
8. What is your Social Insurance Number?
9. What year did you graduate from high school?
10. Have you been arrested before?

If you are faced with these questions during the interview, you could deflect them, prefer not to answer them politely, or ask if they can explain how this question can be relevant to the performance of the job. Questions pertaining to Social Insurance Number, driver's license, criminal history check, etc., could be relevant once the employer is going ahead with an offer or an offer has already been presented.

Rights at Work

Once you start working, you have certain rights as an employee and legal obligations from the employer. Know more about your rights at work by visiting this site. ***www.cplea.ca/rightsatwork**

While wrapping up, thank interviewers, highlight your qualifications, give your closing statement, and mention anything you might have forgotten that is relevant to the role.

Chapter Twelve

Wrapping Up the Interview

As the interview is wrapping up, say a few words of thanks.

The last few minutes are critical and will remain in the minds of the panel even after you have walked out of the interview room. Prepare a closing statement about yourself and say it when wrapping up the meeting. Practice the ending as much as your opening statement. There is a chance that your closing statement will resonate with them even after the interview ends.

This statement should highlight your expertise, what you liked during the interview, and how you would like to contribute to the team. If possible, include points that they might have mentioned about the team. I suggest the following format.

"Thank you for considering me for this position of ______. I appreciate your willingness to share more information about the position and the company. I am particularly interested in this role because ______. I believe this opportunity can enrich both sides. I can bring my expertise in ______, ______, and ______, which will add remarkable value to the team and enhance the position further. I look forward to hearing from you."

This is an opportunity to continue building rapport, thank the interviewers, highlight your qualifications, and mention anything relevant to the role you might have forgotten. This is your last chance to impress the panel.

Ask for the contact information of the interviewers. If they do not have business cards handy, feel free to ask for their email address. You could also look at their LinkedIn profile and reach out to them with a thank you note.

When sending emails, include what you liked about the discussion, potential projects that are coming up, and relevant experience, and emphasize what you can bring to the table to help the company.

Another tip is to take a few thank you cards with you, write a note of thanks, and leave it with the receptionist to forward to the interviewers later. Handwritten notes are more personable than emails. This will show your enthusiasm and interest in the position. It also reminds the interviewer of your qualities and increases your chance of being selected from the candidates they are considering.

While sending an email, ensure that the names, positions, and titles are correctly written. Edit thoroughly to avoid mistakes. Reading from the bottom up is a good idea to capture errors quickly.

Chapter Thirteen

Communication and Language Skills

By Shelley Goldbeck, DTM
(Distinguished Toastmaster)

In one of my career paths, I was a professional recruiter for an international engineering firm. I sought candidates with specific experience and education from all over the world.

It was always thrilling for me to connect with a perfect candidate with all the boxes checked: education, specific tasks completed, and the right specialization!

I recall a specific position I was assigned to fill. We required a specialist with certain geotechnical experience and skills.

And I found the right person for the job!

In the telephone interview, I noticed I had difficulty understanding the candidates' answers. His accent was very strong, and he spoke too quickly.

Because his skills were perfect, I recommended him to the hiring manager. Though he had some difficulty understanding the candidate, he extended an offer of employment, which was accepted.

As was my habit, I followed up with the hiring manager during the probationary period. I learned that the employee had been released.

The hiring manager explained with one word: "Communication."

Without the ability to communicate clearly, the company could not utilize that engineer's "perfect" skills.

This and similar incidents prompted me to investigate possible solutions. It seemed tragic to have to pass over skilled candidates because of a language barrier.

I discovered many staff in my office were frustrated by their inability to effectively communicate because English was their second (or third or fourth) language, or they were unable to understand others with English as a second language.

As a Toastmaster, I was fully cognizant that with a bit of effort, everyone could improve communication skills. So, I resolved to help my colleagues with this specific problem.

Ten volunteers presented themselves to participate in my program. I began by conducting video-recorded assessments, which included a short interview to determine their pronunciation barriers. I learned these obstacles were often specific to each person, depending on their mother tongue. I also discovered some common problems.

Based on the needs identified in the assessments, I created four lessons to help the participants address minor issues.

After only four lessons, all ten participants showed significant improvement in their pronunciation and, therefore, their communication. They also had the awareness required to continue improving.

I learned some important lessons from this experience:

1. With some focus, anyone can improve pronunciation.
2. It's not your fault!
    a. Many people learn English from someone whose own pronunciation is far from perfect.
        i. Often, speakers get "good enough." They can make themselves understood to a point, and they stop improving.
        ii. Nobody tells them that they're saying it incorrectly.
3. Many ESL speakers speak too quickly. It's understandable; once they start thinking in English, they speak as quickly as they would in their mother language. This causes a problem for the listeners; they don't have time to decipher what's being said.

I am pleased to share some tips on improving your English as a second language.

1. Be open to correction. (Some cultures are reluctant to admit any fault. Without that admission, improvement is impossible.)

2. Find a trusted colleague or two with English as a first language to be your speech coach(es). They can hear the sounds that aren't quite right and give you feedback after they've heard you speak in a meeting.

3. Consider joining a Toastmasters International Club. You will get weekly practice with supportive feedback, and you will improve. You might also ask for a mentor or coach within your club.

4. Identify the sounds with which you have the most difficulty. For example, my Spanish-speaking friends have trouble with Vs and Bs, Js, and the *Sh* and *Ch* sounds. (They call me "Chelley!") German, Russian, and speakers of Indo languages have trouble with Vs and Ws. My Chinese friends have issues with Ls and Rs. And almost every person with English as a second language has trouble with the *Th* sounds. When you've identified your problem areas, you can ask your coach to help you with those sounds.

Start with the following two lessons.

1. Lesson One: Slowing Down

   a. The average Texan speaks 40 to 60 words per minute (WPM), while the average Canadian speaks 120 to 140 WPM. In comparison, radio disclaimers are delivered at 300 WPM.

   b. Some people believe that if they speak slowly, they will sound stupid, but it's more important to be understood than to pretend we're smart!

   c. If your pronunciation isn't perfect, you can help your listeners by slowing down.

Here's an easy method to practice speaking slowly.

1. Use a metronome or download a Metronome App. (A metronome is used to help musicians keep their music in time.)
2. Set the metronome to 60 beats per minute.
3. Read a paragraph or story, one word per beat. It will seem ridiculously slow, but it will help you learn to reduce your talking speed, especially when it really matters.
4. This is a tedious exercise, so if you can do five minutes a day, that's a win.
5. Practice until you speak slowly enough to give others time to decipher your words.

2. Lesson Two: *Th*

a. There are two *Th* sounds in the English language, and they do not occur in most other languages. This is why *Th* is most often mispronounced.
b. Stick out your tongue and rest it under your teeth.
c. Now blow air out your mouth. Repeat three times. You've just created the soft or quiet *Th* sound as in "math, theatre, Thursday."
d. To produce the hard or voiced *Th* sound, moan from your voice and feel the vibration of your tongue against your teeth. Examples of the hard or voiced *Th* sound include "this," "father," and "bathe."

e. Create a list of *Th* words and practice reading them daily.

By focusing on these two language improvement exercises, you can significantly improve your communication at work and in the community.

Communication skills are vital in every aspect of life but are especially crucial when searching for work. Developing those skills will pay off in your job search and your ability to stay employed.

I wish you all the best in your journey.

Your network is your net worth.

The connections you make can
lead you to more connections and,
thus, many potential opportunities.

Chapter Fourteen

Job Seeker Resources for New Canadians in Alberta

Immigrating to a new country or city can be daunting and comes with many challenges.

Getting settled into the new city and acclimatizing to a new culture can take several months and even years.

When I was a new Canadian, I struggled to establish a friend circle in the first few years since I was apprehensive about the new environment and culture. Once I got acclimatized to the place, slowly but surely, I made a group of friends I could trust and confide in.

When you first arrive in Canada without friends or family to guide you, the job-hunting process also becomes more taxing.

One of the major tasks ahead of you after arrival is to be gainfully employed. Utilize as many resources as possible to get information about your field of interest and education. Connect with people in the industries you are interested in via social media. Make contacts on professional social media like LinkedIn. Establish a connection with them before asking for help.

Keep your LinkedIn profile current and updated. Highlight your top skills to create a personal brand.

Enhance your summary and headline with a powerful message about your expertise and passion. Ask for positive recommendations from past employers, peers, or mentors.

Recruiters spend a lot of time on social media searching for the ideal candidate, especially after pandemic closures. Contribute on LinkedIn by commenting on good articles and sharing positive messages. Write an article that people in your field can notice and appreciate. Once your connections start noticing your contributions, your network will grow organically.

Here are a few other ways to expand your connections:

- Leverage people in your community and connections from college alumni.
- Reach out to teachers or mentors to check if there are any leads to potential jobs.
- Keep updated with the current labor market trends. Look for information on companies that are expanding, merging, or even opening a new office in town.
- Join a professional organization in your field and attend training, conferences, or trade shows. While attending training, you can learn a new skill that can be added to your resume. Moreover, learning keeps you engaged and motivated during the job search.
- Volunteer in a professional organization in your field. This could open doors to many internal opportunities and build new connections.

- Research the job market and people employed in a similar capacity and understand the necessary certifications to be more employable in your field.
- Reach out to companies that you are interested in. List companies in your field and see if they are hiring. Send a resume to them, even to consider you for future opportunities.
- Connect with key decision-makers in your related field. Ask them for an informational interview or meet over coffee.
- Send your resume to placement agencies. Call them personally and speak with them in detail about your career aspirations. Some positions related to your field may not be posted, but they could be aware of those. Employment experts agree that a significant number of positions do not get posted, and there is a "hidden job market." These positions get filled by networking.
- While speaking to recruiters, mention if you are flexible regarding relocation, fly-in/fly-out, camp, or remote positions.
- Consider contract and temporary positions early on to gain experience and expand your professional network. These contracts have the potential to become long-term positions.
- Answer the common interview questions from Chapter Eight. Role-play the interview with a friend or colleague.
- Joining Toastmasters International is immensely helpful in improving communication and presentation skills. It is a great avenue to network and create a circle of supportive individuals around you.

Toastmasters can help you combat the fear of public speaking and improve your self-confidence. In my experience, improvements happened in speaking and listening.

Your network is your net worth. The connections you make can lead you to more connections and opportunities.

The job scene and work culture might be different from those in other countries. The format of writing resumes can also be different in Canada. Utilize resume writing templates to get help.

Refer to the websites in the Appendix to get guidance in job hunting, interviewing, minimum wage, employment standards, and assessing international qualifications in Canada.

Use these sites as a suggested guideline. Refer to Appendix 2 *

**The Provincial and Federal
Government offers several resources
for newcomers to Canada. Take
advantage of those resources.**

Appendix 1

First Steps for New Canadians in Alberta

After passing many hurdles, when you finally arrive in Canada, there is a huge sigh of relief. Before too long, there is another checklist to complete in order to feel settled in the new land. From applying for a Social Insurance Number and Alberta Health Care Card to finding a family doctor to getting admission to schools, the list goes on. Please see the guidelines to transition smoothly to your new life in Alberta, Canada. (The information mostly pertains to major cities in Alberta, Edmonton, and Calgary.)

Apply for a Social Insurance Number

When you arrive in Canada, one of the first things to do is apply for a Social Insurance Number (SIN). You will require this nine-digit number to open a bank account, access any government programs, and obtain employment.

Apply Online for a SIN: sin-nas.canada.ca/en/Sin/

Apply for Health Care (AHCIP)

In order to access universal health care and obtain access to hospitals, clinics, etc., apply for Alberta Health Care Insurance.

Apply online for AHCIP: www.alberta.ca/ahcip-how-to-apply.aspx#toc-2

In order to apply, you have to provide supporting documents such as:

- Legal entitlement to live in Canada

- Identity
- Residency

Alberta Health Care services cover hospital visits. It does not cover prescription drugs or specialized services like physiotherapy or dental care, which are covered by most employers.

All newcomers must have their own health care card, including minors. You will need to present them in order to access medical services.

Apply for a Driver's License

To obtain a driver's license, apply online: **www.alberta.ca/get-drivers-licence-steps.aspx**

Driver's Knowledge Test: www.alberta.ca/drivers-knowledge-test.aspx

Driver's Road Test: www.alberta.ca/drivers-road-test.aspx

Class 7 Learner's License www.alberta.ca/class-7-learners-licence.aspx

Exchange a license from outside Alberta: www.alberta.ca/exchange-non-alberta-licences.aspx

Canada Child and Family Benefits

The Canada Child Benefit (CCB) is administered by the Canada Revenue Agency (CRA). It is a tax-free monthly payment made to eligible families to help with the cost of raising children under 18 years of age.

To apply online: **www.canada.ca/en/revenue-agency/services/child-family-benefits/canada-child-benefit-overview.html**

Education

New student enrolment in Calgary schools:
www.cbe.ab.ca/registration/registration/Pages/default.
aspx

New student enrolment in Edmonton schools:
epsb.ca/schools/register/newstudentregistration/

Transportation

The transit websites provide information on fares,
transit passes, subsidies for low-income, bus schedules,
routes, and city maps. They also allow users to plan
trips and estimate travel time to a location.

Calgary Transit: www.calgarytransit.com/

Edmonton Transit: www.edmonton.ca/edmonton-
transit-system-ets.aspx

Finding Walk-In Clinics

Calgary: medimap.ca/Location/Calgary
Edmonton: medimap.ca/Location/Edmonton

Renting and Housing

This is a guide to the rental process, providing
tenants and landlords with an overview of their rights
and responsibilities as well as handy worksheets,
sample letters, and helpful hints. Provincial and
territorial contacts and fact sheets are also included.

Renter insurance is available to safeguard your
valuables in the event of a contingency (fire, flooding,
burglary, etc.)

www.cmhc-schl.gc.ca/en/buying/condominium-
buyers-guide/provincial-fact-sheets/alberta-fact-sheet_

For Renters: www.cmhc-schl.gc.ca/en/rental-
housing

Finding Rentals in Calgary:

- www.rentfaster.ca/ab/calgary

- calgary.rentspot.com
- 4rent.ca/Rent-Calgary-113/listing/
- rentals.ca/calgary
- www.bwalk.com/en-ca/rent/search/alberta/calgary

Centre for Newcomers, Calgary

The Centre for Newcomers offers settlement services, job and career advice, and English language training.

www.centrefornewcomers.ca

The City of Calgary

The city offers resources to assist newcomers in settling in. The site also has a list of culturally diverse organizations.

www.calgary.ca/CSPS/CNS/Pages/Immigrants-newcomers-and-refugees/Helping-newcomers-get-started-in-Calgary.aspx

The City of Edmonton

This site offers germane information about municipal services, transit, housing, multi-cultural communities, libraries, and settlement services.

www.edmonton.ca/programs_services/documents/Newcomers_Guide_English_FINAL.pdf

CCIS (Calgary Catholic Immigration Society)

The CCIS is a non-profit organization that provides settlement and integration services to all immigrants and refugees in Southern Alberta. www.ccisab.ca

YMCA

The YMCA works with over 320 high school and young adults each year who are new to Canada. The

YMCA also offers English language classes for newcomers to Canada.

www.ymcacalgary.org/community-ymca/newcomer-programs/

The Immigrant Education Society

The immigrant education society helps newcomers and their families by providing simplified solutions to complex life problems.

www.immigrant-education.ca

CIWA (Calgary Immigrant Women's Association)

CIWA, a registered charity and non-profit organization, offers programs and services to women such as integration programs, learning support services, career services for foreign-trained professionals, financial coaching, childcare training, etc. www.ciwa-online.com

Immigrant Services Calgary (ISC)

As a non-profit organization, Immigrant Services Calgary facilitates a smooth transition and successful integration into the Calgary community. They ensure newcomers have access to programs and services such as translation, career support, and family counseling. These services can help newcomers overcome the challenges that come with immigrating to a new country, thus setting them up to succeed in their new life in Canada.

www.immigrantservicescalgary.ca/settlement-support

Calgary Library

Newcomers can find Canadian Citizenship and English language proficiency tests such as IELTS and TOFEL.

calgarylibrary.ca/read-learn-and-explore/digital-library/learning-express

Visit Calgary –www.visitcalgary.com

Explore Edmonton – exploreedmonton.com

The City of Edmonton

This site offers relevant information about municipal services, transit, housing, multi-cultural communities, libraries, and settlement services.

www.edmonton.ca/programs_services/documents/Newcomers_Guide_English_FINAL.pdf

Financial Planning

Here are major banks with their newcomer web pages.

RBC: www.rbc.com/newcomers/#just-arrived

TD: www.td.com/ca/en/personal-banking/solutions/new-to-canada/

CIBC: newcomer.cibc.com/new-to-canada

BMO: www.bmo.com/main/personal/newcomers-to-canada/

Here's access to better financial planning, including building credit for the future to get loans, mortgages, etc. www.moneysense.ca/save/financial-planning/getting-started *

The links to all websites were working at the time of writing. The author is not responsible for changes to the links or websites.

Appendix 2

Refer to the following websites to get guidance in job hunting, interviewing, minimum wage, employment standards, and assessing international qualifications in Canada. Use these sites as a suggested guideline. *

Job Search Sites

www.indeed.ca

www.workopolis.com

www.monster.ca

Average Pay Scale in Canada

www.payscale.com

Laws on Minimum Wage and Employment Standards

www.alberta.ca/employment-standards.aspx

Employment & Translation Services:

www.immigrantservicescalgary.ca/

IQAS International Qualifications Assessment Service

www.alberta.ca/iqas-overview.aspx

Licensing Bodies for Regulated Professions in Canada

Professions such as medical, accounting, dental practices, etc., are regulated by licensing bodies in Canada.

See the websites of some licensing bodies: *

Accounting
- www.cpacanada.ca
- www.cpaalberta.ca

Dental
- http://www.cda-adc.ca/cdacweb/en/
- ndeb-bned.ca/en
- www.dentalhealthalberta.ca

Dietary
- www.dietitians.ca/Become-a-Dietitian/Registration-to-Practice.aspx
- http://www.collegeofdietitians.ab.ca

Doctors/Physicians
- http://www.cpsa.ca

Engineering and Geosciences
- www.apega.ca
- www.aset.ab.ca

Human Resources
- www.cphrab.ca

Information Technology
- www.cipsalberta.ca

Law
- flsc.ca/national-committee-on-accreditation-nca/
- www.lawsociety.ab.ca

Nursing
- www.cna-aiic.ca/en/nursing-practice/the-practice-of-nursing/regulation-of-rns/rn-exam
- www.clpna.com

Occupational Therapy
- caot.ca
- acot.ca

Pharmacy
- www.pharmacists.ca

- abpharmacy.ca

Physiotherapy
- www.alliancept.org
- www.physiotherapyalberta.ca

Social Work
- www.cswe.org
- caswe-acfts.ca/home/
- www.acsw.ab.ca/site/home

Trades and Journeymen
- tradesecrets.alberta.ca

Veterinary
- abvma.ca

Conclusion

This book provides you with a plethora of tips and tools to improve your confidence level, structure your answers effectively, and perform better in interviews overall.

I believe each person is gifted with a unique talent and is an expert in at least one thing. Discover your own gifts, fine-tune them, and perfect them. It is important to focus on your strengths rather than your improvement areas.

While moving forward, take small steps toward self-improvement. Your changes will come gradually, not overnight. Promise yourself to keep trying meticulously, one day at a time, until you ace it. Write down your goals, vision, and values. Take at least one action per day to achieve your goals. Aim for perfect progress, not perfection.

Utilize your talents not only for your benefit but also for the people around you. You rise while lifting others.

"The purpose of life is not to be happy. It is to be useful, to be honorable, to be compassionate, to have it make some difference that you have lived and lived well."
- Ralph Waldo Emerson.

Though the road is narrow and winding, eventually, you will reach your destination.

The interview conversations could be a game changer in your career. A new career can bring better opportunities, lifestyle, and financial benefits. Choose a career you are passionate about in order to have a fulfilling career rather than working for money. Money is a consequence of what you do passionately.

My reward is tenfold when I am able to help individuals fulfill their full potential and find their right career path.

-Leena Mary Alex

Acknowledgments

I am deeply grateful to everyone who has supported me throughout the creation of this book, through their kind words, testimonials, and insightful suggestions.

A heartfelt thanks to my family, whose unwavering inspiration has been a constant source of strength in my journey. I also appreciate everyone who has motivated me with their words, actions, and prayers.

A special thank you to Shelley Goldbeck for her valuable contribution of a chapter on communication.

About the Author
Leena Mary Alex, CPHR, MBA

Leena's experience spans over 20 years in human resources, specifically in recruitment and retention strategies. She has worked in industries such as manufacturing, staffing, regulatory, pipelines and oil and gas, during which she gained a wealth of knowledge in behavioral-based interviews, coaching, mentoring, and facilitating. This gave her exposure to various styles of recruitment and a broad spectrum of roles.

As a passionate Toastmaster, she has served as a mentor, coach, VP, and President, Area Director and Division Director of Toastmasters in Calgary.

www.linkedin.com/in/leenaalex
Leena@TalentSuccess.ca
www.TalentSuccess.ca

About Contributing Author
Shelley Goldbeck, DTM

Shelley is a thinker, writer, speaker, and entertainer who has enjoyed a varied and interesting career in sales, marketing, human resources, real estate, and other fields.

She currently works as a consultant, helping others improve their lives and businesses by drawing from her many years of experience.

ShelleyGoldbeck@gmail.com
www.ShelleyGoldbeck.com

9 781069 330604

www.ingramcontent.com/pod-product-compliance
Lightning Source LLC
Chambersburg PA
CBHW071458030726
47593CB00003B/1051